The Gloucester Fragments

Poems

Neil Leadbeater

Littoral Press

First Published in 2022 by:
Littoral Press, 15 Harwood Place
Lavenham, Sudbury, Suffolk CO10 9SG

©Neil Leadbeater
©Cover Photograph Caroline Gill

ISBN 978-1-912412-40-2

British Library Cataloguing-in-Publication Data:
A catalogue record of this book is available from
The British Library

Printed and bound in Great Britain by:
4Edge Ltd. Hockley, Essex
www.4edge.co.uk

for Jane

Acknowledgements

The author is grateful to the editors of the following publications in which some of these poems, a few in earlier versions, have appeared:

Dreich, Ink Pantry, Littoral Magazine, Orizont Literar Contemporan (Romania), *Ovi Magazine* (Finland), *Poetry Plus, Quill & Parchment* (USA) and *The Bond Street Review* (USA).

An earlier version of 'St Luke's Little Summer' and sections of 'The Cheltenham Slides' appeared in the World Poetic and Artistic Anthology (editura pim, Iaşi, Romania, 2021).

Special thanks are due to Caroline Gill for permission to reproduce her photograph of a redwing and to Lori Levy and Polly Stretton for their comments on my work. Thanks are also due to the Burgh Poets, Stirling, who provided me with helpful commentary and encouragement when some of these poems were still in their infancy.

About the Author:

Neil Leadbeater is an author, essayist, poet and critic living in Edinburgh, Scotland. His work has been published widely in anthologies and journals both at home and abroad. His publications include *Librettos for the Black Madonna* (White Adder Press, 2011); *The Worcester Fragments* (Original Plus, 2013); *The Loveliest Vein of Our Lives* (Poetry Space, 2014); *The Fragility of Moths* (editura pim, Iaşi, Romania, 2014); *Sleeve Notes* (editura pim, Iaşi, Romania,, 2016); *Brasilia* (co-authored with Monica Manolachi) (editura pim, Iaşi, Romania,, 2019); *Penn Fields* (Littoral Press, 2019); *Reading Between the Lines* (Littoral Press, 2020) and *Journeys in Europe* (co-authored with Monica Manolachi) (Bifrost, 2022, Bucharest, Romania). His work has been translated into several languages. He is a regular reviewer for a number of journals including *The Halo Halo Review* (USA); *Quill & Parchment* (USA); *The High Window* (UK), *The Poet* (UK) and *Write Out Loud* (UK).

Contents:

I: Rivers Breaking into Song

Rivers in the Dorian Mode

In that see-saw Margery Daw
ocean of a morning,
red poll bullocks near a barbed wire fence
steer clear of the flood -
all that collective improvisation
driven by the height of tides –
not the happy-go-lucky flow
you sometimes see in summer -
but one that shifts into
a faster pace -
an orchestral outburst
of tidal manoeuvres
surging up from the Channel –
so we listen to fenders
shielding blows
that, and the willows weeping.

Plumbing the Depths of River Water /
The Severn at Wainlode

This afternoon we set to work
beside the red bank
and the dipple-dapple river
stirring up with Severn shafts
sumps of mud and gravel,
bottles, gaffing irons,
throwaway goods,
Lydney coal whose black slack
would not let go of the past.

In the distance
we made out common fumitory –
a mass of grey that looked like smoke
as it scrambled for a footing.

Up close, it smouldered
with resentment
having to jostle for a premium space
with vigorous bramble
and bindweed.

Everything has to find its place
on land or in the water.

Calliope

Fairground music. The carousel in full swing
dizzying the horses. And over the fence,
ruminants tearing at grass. What do they make
of the steam whistles, Fuller's band
sounding in their ears or this vision of Adonis,
caught between the merry-go-round and
the juggling act: Aphrodite on one side,
Persephone on the other? Some of us
made a song and dance about it.
No need to let it reach epic proportions
it's just a spat, we said, but baby,
one eye on the cows, wauls among
the coconut shies, not so sure.

Circe

One by one you changed us into wolves,
lions, swine. Our bodies
became four-footed,
as we shrieked our vocals into the air,
bellowed in open country,
caged in zoos and sties.

We have been shape-shifted
through sorcery
scaring the wits out of loved ones
who do not understand.

The River in a Horseshoe Bend / Minsterworth Meadows

Standing on the outer curve
you wonder what lies beneath –
picture skeletons of wicker funnels
woven with hazel and withy,
lave nets, eel spears,
oars of oak…
or think of pear blossom
on Minsterworth Meadows,
a haven for reed mace and yellow flag
that, and the periwinkle,
racing through hedgerows
as if on a mission
to break all records
at so many yards per year.

Nodens

The Severn has its own god, a god of health and healing,
a god of good luck. And there's a baying hound
in him somewhere, a symbol of restoration
throughout the classical world.
You can see him on temple floors
surrounded by salmon and sea serpents
(more probably conger eels)
or riding at Lydney on a horse-drawn chariot
accompanied by Tritons with coracle paddles
galloping over fields.

Such are the visions of those from the past
who believe it still in their dreams.

Churn

Here, where seven springs of leap-water
flow beneath the trees
it carves a niche through a wooded gorge
to place-names beginning with 'C' –
Cubberley, Cowley, Colesborne and Cerney;
Cirencester too, 'the Capital of the Cotswolds' –
its rippling nonchalance a quiet alliteration
of riverine sounds –
'purling' to you and me.

Poem for the Windrush

With much to explore
and youth on your side
you have all the time
to chunter -
to rub shoulders
with pebble beds
and leave no stone
unturned.

At Coln Rogers

The day we went to Coln Rogers
roads shaded by hedgerows
were dense with greater bindweed,
hemp agrimony and
purple loosestrife
and in the flat, floodable meadows,
the spotted fritillaries
were doing their rounds
in the deep hours of June.

The out-of-control weather
too hot to handle
made us argumentative.
Even the foxgloves were fractious,
their bell-shaped flowers
x-rated for sex appeal
thrilled with the noise of bees.

We stepped back, kept our distance,
fearful of being stung.

Caught in the Rain at Awre

How many times does it rain in the psalms?
Seven times or seventy times seven?
Forgive me for asking
but several warnings are now in place
at Severn Ham and Tewkesbury,
Chaceley and Haw Bridge,
Apperley and The Leigh.
The river is trespassing all over the land
at Ashleworth and Wyman's Brook
putting the spa at risk.
Northway Lane is closed in both directions
and 4 x 4's are making waves
on roads around our town. There are no
Noahs here, no factories in which to build
a lightweight, watertight ark.
Farmers are out looking to bring
livestock into shelter. Insurance
is pouring over a torrent of print
to define an 'Act of God'.
A deluge of claims (unstoppable)
is now flooding in.

Where do we go from here?
Solving that issue
brings the army and the fire brigade
clothed in their distinct apparel
rowing over the fields.

II: Slad Valley Landscapes, Seasons and Songs

A Poem in the Wake of Autumn's Furrow

is a poem whose lines
have been worked by gulls
after the baler has
spread its load
and the tractor
has turned
in the bottom field -
everything
set for winter.

Astronomical Autumn

The extent of it. Do you ever think for a second
how everything mellows in the dying light –
the barbed remark of the nettle
softening its impact after brittle hairs
have injected their hypodermics,
the leaves letting go, saying goodbye,
'so long' after all this time.

Anyone for Coffee?

Coffee, (which makes the politician wise,
And see thro' all things with his half-shut eyes)...

-Pope, The Rape of the Lock.

In Caffe Corretto, Hubble Bubble
or the March Hare,
('very nice, thank you'),
'X' lobs questions over the net.
Fired up by bagels, coffee
and breadsticks
he confounds his opponent
with a cross court shot
Greek, Georgian or Turkish
always to his advantage.

His sparring partner
dazzles to impress with a rising shot
of Sumatran Blue Mandheling.

Game, set and match.

An Incident in the Library

So what does it mean
'to throw the book at someone'?
Books are not meant to be thrown –
they should be handled with care,
especially the Penguin Modern Poets.
Throw them
and you ruin their jackets,
or worse, fracture their spines.

The gods had other ways
to express displeasure:
Artemis turned Actaeon into a deer
Zeus bound Ixion to a burning wheel,
while Apollo flayed Marsyas
then turned him into a stream.
In anyone's book,
these would be deemed 'severe'
so you pick up the volume
you hurled in anger,
mutter an apology,
and leave.

Astronomical Winter

The depth of it. Ambuscades of snow
sleet the counterpane. The child in
the nursery, master of his own world,
shakes the globe. Whipping flakes
into a perfect storm, he sends the snowman
with his red scarf and standing brush
into a state of oblivion.

Outside, the Colorado beetle, who knows
nothing of this, keeps himself
in the dark.

Children Exercising in a School Yard

Years back I journeyed through
the same routine -
a parabola on a graph of air:

Stand at ease: stand easy.

'The village pump' –
one arm snaking down the left-hand side
as far as an arm can go
and then the repeat on the other side.

Stand at ease: stand easy.

'The windmill' –
arms flying to the left and right
sails driven by wind

Stand at ease: stand easy.

Press-ups on a count to twenty
or lying down with your legs in the air
is a form of art for life.
'Drill' we called it,
as we poured out of maths,
contorting our bodies
into geometric shapes:

Stand at ease: stand easy.

Indoors, wide awake and raring to go,
we romped through French imperatives

like we never did before:
étendez-vous! levez-vous! asseyez-vous!
lie down! get up! sit down!

Demonstratives

On a point of grammar
demonstrative pronouns and determiners
are singular *this* and *that*
and plural *these* and *those.*

You should know, however,
that they love to show off
as in 'this Alfa Romeo Spider Veloci
can really do a ton
on straight country roads' or
'those John Deere tractors
exceed expectation with their
high performance and reliability:
take it from me –
I've driven one'

That's how we learnt our pronouns
the day Mr. Reid chalked up
our superlatives. He had a way
of building us up, taught us
to lead by example.

Possessives

There's always something personal
about these pronouns.
Jealousy climbs into bed with them,
all that bitterness
about bureau bookcases
and pedestal desks...

we've seen it all before.

Interrogatives

Those days we could use interrogatives like
Did I tell you about the heatwave in July?
and get a Yes /No answer
without alarming the young
about global warming
because we would watch the question trail off
into a deckchair lethargy of long afternoons
spent under trees loaded with fruit
not yet ready to fall.

Errata for an English Pangram

for	a	read	the
for	slow	read	quick
for	black	read	brown
for	cat	read	fox
for	slinks	read	jumps
for	under	read	over
for	a	read	the
for	wire	read	lazy
for	fence	read	dog

Astronomical Spring

The rite of it. When March blunders
into the copse and lions turn into
lambs: Flora's dancing daffodils
laughing off the breeze.
Conversations *tete à tete*
about the depth of yellow,
Lydia Sokolova
and her fine balletic poise.

Ivor

Not one for conversation,
I drove him to St. Mary de Lode
to see the stained glass window
and watched him stand in silence
as if trying to look
through a glass darkly
afraid of what he might find.

Everything set him on edge:
an enemy crouching behind a column
the sound of a door closing,
someone's cough and its loud acoustic,
a dropped hymnal
that made him jump
right out of his mind.

Leaving Stroud

As I walked out, I didn't think twice
that midsummer morning about leaving behind
John Apperley's mills.

Coming out of the Slad Valley
my thoughts were far from the lawnmower
and the adjustable spanner,
the green baize cloth on the snooker table,
citadels of stone.

So what if I was running late?

I had everything I needed in my kit bag
a fortune slung on my shoulder.

Astronomical Summer

The height of it. And high summer
has yet to come. Meteorologists
say temperatures will continue to rise
but cups buttering the meadow
are still in their infancy and
the lazy daisy has yet to spill
its petals to the light.
Days grow longer for dreaming in.
There are possibilities
in the Swells and the Slaughters,
cloud in the Stroudwater Hills.
Jessica puts on her party frock
and cows jump over the moon.

Ceres

Surely these poppies raised by farmers
for their stems and seeds
are a part of her iconography?

She said to me once, 'at least credit me
with the discovery of spelt wheat,
the yoking of oxen and ploughing…'
And I had to concur but drew the line
at letting out the foxes,
hoping to find a better way
to shield the crop from vermin.

Yarley Meadows

In textbooks
they lie on Jurassic and Cretaceous clays –
are a part of the Denchworth Series –
'slow, permeable soils'
good for winter cereals.

This morning
you are doing your Darcey Bussell bit
though it's hard to pirouette
on saturated ground.

I watch you lapwing like a young girl
testing the twirl of your dress
until you proclaim you are done with it
giddy with meadows
whirling off-centre
then coming together
catching you up
as I give you my round of applause.

III: Places North and West

At St. Kenelm's Well

By Salter's Hill,
in Ivor Gurney's
full June blaze
we found the wellhouse
which is Winchcombe's
best kept secret.

Years back
when we lowered
our buckets for water
doves came up
with laurel leaves
and dazzled us
with their whiteness

but there are no birds today
just the miracle
of a Red Admiral
opening and closing
its wings.

Elegy for a Disused Quarry

At Stenders, this quarry lets slip
that its fossiliferous limestone shales
are the best in the Forest of Dean
'where junctions with the Old Red Sandstone
and part of the Lower Dolomite formation
are visible to the naked eye'.

What a
b
   l   s
      a   t !

But I'd rather put it in plain English –
say how rocks have yielded up fossils,
the remains of sea lilies, shellfish, fleas…

It's like lifting the dustsheet
off an old bed frame
then seeing the mattress below
a patterning of
springs and coils
stripped down to this.

Following a Line of Offa's Dyke

On St. Briavel's Common
between the ridge summit and the eastern fringe
of Hudnall's Wood:
these boundaries.
Earthworks chasing a line of the Wye:
their course through woodland
marked by yews
where a glint of sun from an unseen greenhouse
suddenly catches the eye.

As children, we were always on the lookout
for the next Viking invasion,
talked how we would stare them down
petrify them into standing stones
strewn upon the ground.

But sheep nudging at meadow grass
seem peaceful enough for now.
It is they who know the lie of the land
right down to the basics,
its richest, darkest soil.

Mapping the Frampton Flora

Finding them in the open glade
was almost dreamlike –
sisters who shared a passion
for Severnside flowers
in Stancombe woods and fields –
ground ivy
that was 'runaway Jack'
and early purple orchids
which the girls called
'goosey-ganders'
Kowalksi's Dancing Maidens
caught in the glare of June.

Frampton Pools

are pockets of standing water:
pits quarried for gravel -
a stopping-off point for winter-visiting shoveler
and great-crested grebe.
Octobers are their rush hour
the time when Frampton B&Bs are
full to the brim with twitter,
the live exchange of bird chatter
that shrills down the wire:

NO VACANCIES.

The Early Arrival of Flowers

Bunched against the fickle frost
she found them –
a plethora of miniature
fragrant clusters
blushing in abundance.
Charlotte was jealous
of the dozen or so primulas
popping up out of the damp earth
mid-winter. Quixotic
she called it –
a gesture whose need to be seen
could fill a room with extravagance.
How did they do it?
It was some kind of secret
she would tilt at windmills for.
The girl was beside herself.
The way they had snaked
mellow-yellow
into her long line of sight
filling her head with surprise
like that
had been a real zinger.

Lambs Leaping

Startled by the Cheltenham Express
racing through the vale
they make a dash for cover.

When you are young
there is always somewhere to run to.

June and the Art of Leg Spin Bowling

East of Bishopston
the old men of Ashley Down
inherit the high ground.
Their sights are on the match:
a one day international.

It is June.

Summer, still in its infancy,
has not yet reached its sultry state
and there is everything left to play for.

The leg breaks come fast and furious –
balls bowled right-arm
with a wrist spin action
that swerve from right
to left when they bounce down
hard on the ground.

They watch the stumps
fly from the pitch.
A five wicket fall in a single innings
from B. S. Chandrasekhar
is the kind of success
they are looking for.

It's all down to delivery –
the amount of side spin
versus the top spin:
a ball's trajectory
looping through air.

Guests Leaving The Bell

A Study in Movement and Stasis

It all happens before ten. Rules
By Order of The Management
insist upon it. Their departure,
in dribs and drabs, has purpose.
We watch them from the café
trailing their luggage behind them.
We wonder where they are going,
where they are off to next. Restless,
they will not settle until they reach
the next stage in their journey.

**Gustav Holst Considers a Pebble
While Composing 'The Planets'.**

He cradles its convexities
in the palm of his hand,
feels its significance,
weighs its bulk.

Striated it could be Saturn,
whose drawn lines
are deeply scarred
from hard-earned experience.

Pockmarked with craters,
it could have been Mars.

Cold, it could be Neptune.

Its sudden jollity
is the playfulness of Jupiter.

Broken open
he hears music.

How did it get inside?

The Cheltenham Slides

Maloney on Silver Fame, Sherwood on Desert Orchid, McGuire on Cool Ground and Jonson on Looks Like Trouble...

(i)

Cobbett called it 'a resort of the lame and the lazy, the gormandizing and the guzzling, the bilious and the nervous.'

He must have missed the Montpelier Promenade on a fine summer's day.

(ii)

In 'the city of magnificent distances' we have all the space in the world.

(iii)

The town's changed. All places do.

Now its hooves pounding turf, bookies shouting the odds.

(iv)

Lightweight ballistic and blast resistant armour panels for tanks and military vehicles followed by Cotswold scenery (they can't tow that away)

and lastly, landing gear
are what this spa is known for.
Every plane you've flown on
has had to let down its wheels
just like this poem
coming in to land
lays down its lines and ends.

The Wilson Galleries

The galleries invite us to *Explore, Discover, be Curious*.
Their exteriors are an eclectic mix of architectural styles
aesthetically 'bolted on' to what was once
the Regency original.

Inside we head for De Ferrière
and then to Archaeology for a display of
hooks and shears.

The distraction of children is appealing.
The attendant seems oblivious
to girls doing cartwheels
across the gallery floor –
she, too, was young once.

A school party moves in. Their shrill voices carry far,
are heard before they are seen.
The teachers make them sit like angels
to draw down on paper
imagination's wings.

Their enthusiasm is palpable.
They are not afraid of making mistakes,
of getting things out of proportion.
There are no winners or losers,
just art for art's sake.

At what age does a fear of failure
begin to take its hold?

In Fine Art,
we are drawn to a Nash engraving;
Turner's 'Cook's Folly, River Avon, Bristol'
and Thornton's 'Hill Farm, Painswick' –
an oil on canvas
where corn is flooded in sunlight,
and buildings lie beyond.

Later in the Café
we reflect on what we have seen:

paintings spanning four centuries
oriental collections of pottery,
archaeological treasures
from the Cotswold escarpment
and a room devoted to Wilson
that esteemed son of Cheltenham
who perished en route to the South Pole
in the year 1912.

The Double Gloucesters

That August,
at the Agricultural Society's
Annual Show
you saw the great cheeses:
DAIRY PRODUCE writ large
the full-fat variety
made from the milk of
Gloucester cattle.
You wanted to savour
the whole churn of them,
the swirling, wheel-shaped
vat of them,
right there on your tongue.

Hard-pressed to declare
a winner, judges could not
praise enough their rich,
nutty mellow flavours,
their apricot
Lady's bedstraw yellow,
that mix of milk and cream.

Poem in the Vale of Leadon

In the Redmarley Hills, a mile from the county boundary,
I think of the Dymock poets:
Frost at Little Iddles, Abercrombie in Ryton
Gibson in Bromgreen,
and see the beech trees with their gun-barrel trunks
where farmsteads spring surprises…
It's just another vista
that shifts us into a new perspective
swapping sunlight for a canopy of shade:
the slipping seasons that drive us on
to our own allotted ends.

St Martin's Little Summer

It happens mid-November
after the fireworks
have jumped their jacks
and rockets launched from bottles
have fallen short of the moon –
a week of warmth
for the old ones
and always
at the edge of the field
a seated saint
who offers his coat
to a stranger
in need of clothes.

The Winchcombe Meteorite

It's not often you find the debris
of a 4.6 billion year old meteorite
in your driveway,
its flight captured by six camera networks
of the UK Fireball Alliance
and the doorbell cameras
of private dwellings.

That February
when it blazed over western England
before coming down to Earth
it was bored with circling
the solar nebula
so it decided to go AWOL
just like Ivuna, Alais and Flensburg.

Considering its age,
it took its time

a
r
r
i
v
i
n
g

IV: All Points East

'All the birds of Oxfordshire and Gloucestershire'

Hyperbole: noun. An exaggerated statement or claim not meant to be taken literally.

Listen, he couldn't have heard them all.
The wren's blue-sky thinking
could have outwitted him
and then there was the chiffchaff
who flew out of the copse
before the train had slowed to its stop.
That clearing of the throat
would have drowned out the robin
who flew off the fork handle
when he saw the station master cross the line
but it was all or nothing that day
no half-measures were allowed.

The County Limes

What kind they were, small-leaved
large-leaved or a crossbreed of the two,
I can't recall. Strung in columnar rows
they could have squandered fields,
been planted as windbreaks,
lost themselves in vast woods
fighting for the light,
instead they are streetwise.
Fending off axes laid at the root,
they have the measure of us
in their DNA, our seasons
in their rings.

Driving Through the Lights at Lechlade

was how you never got to know the place
that was your excuse
when the light was green
you exulted in it
putting your foot down
in the MGM sports car
as if there was no time to lose with living
and plenty more to come.

Hello Young Plovers

Hello young plovers whoever you are
flying in plovery skies –
it feels like
I'm getting to know you.

Hello to you
coming in to land,
where you are from
is a puzzlement.

Hello to you
who are passing through:
welcome to the
garden rendezvous.

Do you read me? /
Over.

A Street in Northleach

Not Lowry's 'Street' which is 'The Green'
set in the bitter winter of 1947
with children playing in the snow,
but 'The Peep' –
68 metres in length
with its own unique reference number
in the National Street Gazetteer.
Being a major wool town
I tried to find a narrow opening,
a surreptitious link
and came up with 'Bo Peep'
who lost her sheep
and didn't know where to find them.

It was either that or chickens.

Hollyhocks

are the jolly hockey sticks of kitchen gardens,
midfielders who stand attentive
a cut above the rest
because they love it when a poem like this
goes out on a limb
to chase an image across a pitch
and then return it
red side up
with a blazing side-line hit.

Mangolds

Today we watched the farmhands shovel the roots
into a box on the lifter. Fodder crop
for livestock in the flatlands
of Gloucester,
the shine on the leaves
already dulled
the globes piled high like cannon-shot
in pits, hogs and pies.

At Calcot Farm, Coln St. Dennis

*At Calcot Farm in 1948 Professor Talbot Rice introduced the poll
variety of Hereford cattle to Britain.*

This is where they slipped in,
medium to rich red
with white markings on the face,
brisket, neckline, crest,
switch and legs (below the knees and hocks).

Possessing a typically large,
muscular red frame,
how could the white-faced officials
have missed them
at Passport Control…
or did they just wave them through
as if on a whim…
business as usual?

Queen Anne's Lace

In the nook of Wyck we saw you
Williams' wild carrot
taking the fields by force
your small blooms, dull white,
clustered in dense flat umbels:
Dresden lace on a cambric ground,
Venetian point with a coarse thread,
refined Brazilian 'Sols'.

St. Luke's Little Summer

Heat breaks
through a line of russets
calm as a
running tide.

Our hope of it lasting
is as thin as a grass-blade
but sometimes the doctor,
mid-October,
gifts to us
these days.

Coln St. Aldwyns

In 1953, 'Gardener's Question Time'
with Franklin Engelmann
came here. The programme was recorded
in the Village Hall (now defunct)
by the BBC.

I was two years old.

I have a shrub that doesn't want to flower.
(but not all shrubs do!)
How do I identify my soil type?
(clay, silt, peat or chalk?)
How can I get rid of slugs?
(you never will).
Is it safe to move my peony?
(yes, but it won't like it).
Can you suggest some plants
that will grow in the shade?
(snowdrops, dog tooth violets,
hydrangeas, hostas
and the hart's tongue fern).
How can I attract bees?
(foxgloves)....

Between the Norman church
and the cottage gardens
these same questions
year after year.

Your Daughter Lost in Summer Heat

Among the mullioned windows,
grey stone tiles and
dormered gables
you found her
'threading the eye of a needle'
through Poppett's Alley,
before the reality
that she was totally lost had registered
in her face.
Suddenly the High Street was beautiful
the noonday sun more brilliant,
the lichen-mottled stonework of Chipping Campden
more alive than ever
such was your joy at finding her
as you cradled her in your arms
and held back the tears
away from the gaze
of all you ever loved.

Notes on the Poems

Some of the material in the first section, 'Rivers Breaking into Song' has been derived from 'Severn Tide', a study of the upper part of the tidal estuary of the Severn, by Brian Waters (J.M. Dent & Sons, 1947, reprinted 1955). Some of the material for the other sections has been inspired by a reading of R. P. Beckinsale's 'Companion into Gloucestershire' (Methuen, 1944 edition) and Richard Mabey's 'The Frampton Flora' (Guild Publishing, 1985 edition).

Calliope: This poem was inspired in part by a reading of John Fuller's poem 'Band Music' in his collection 'Fairground Music' (The Phoenix Living Poets / Chatto and Windus with The Hogarth Press, 1961).

Caught in the Rain at Awre: The place-name is pronounced like the letter 'R'. The reference to the psalms relates to the fact that Thomas Sternhold, (d. 1549), who teamed up with John Hopkins (d. 1570) to produce the first metrical version of the psalms, may have been born at Awre although this is by no means certain.

Anyone for Coffee? The entire poem is composed out of terminology used in relation to the game of tennis.

Astronomical Spring: The English ballerina, Lydia Sokolova (not her real name), was a prominent member of Sergei

Diaghilev's Ballets Russes from 1913 to 1929. Her most famous role was that of the Chosen Maiden in Léonide Massine's reworking of Igor Stravinsky's ballet 'The Rite of Spring'.

Ivor: In 2000, a stained glass window was installed in St. Mary de Lode Church, Gloucester and dedicated to the memory of the English poet and composer, Ivor Gurney (1890-1937).

Leaving Stroud: The subject of the poem is the poet, novelist and screenwriter, Laurie Lee (1914-1999). Stroud was the place where Edwin Beard Budding invented the lawnmower and the adjustable spanner. It is also the place where green baize cloth used to cover snooker tables is made.

The Early Arrival of Flowers: This poem was written in response to a word prompt in which at least 22 given words had to be utilised.

Hello Young Plovers: This poem mentions several song titles from Rogers and Hammerstein's musical 'The King and I'.

Hollyhocks: This poem is composed out of terminology used in relation to the game of hockey.